AF269427

IRELAND

R.L. Van

Big Buddy Books
An Imprint of Abdo Publishing
abdobooks.com

abdobooks.com

Published by Abdo Publishing, a division of ABDO, PO Box 398166, Minneapolis, Minnesota 55439.
Copyright © 2023 by Abdo Consulting Group, Inc. International copyrights reserved in all countries. No part of this book may be reproduced in any form without written permission from the publisher. Big Buddy Books™ is a trademark and logo of Abdo Publishing.

Printed in the United States of America, North Mankato, Minnesota
102022
012023

THIS BOOK CONTAINS RECYCLED MATERIALS

Design: Emily O'Malley, Mighty Media, Inc.
Production: Mighty Media, Inc.
Editor: Jessica Rusick
Cover Photograph: Eugen B/Shutterstock Images
Interior Photographs: Alla Laurent/Shutterstock Images, p. 6 (middle); ASUWAN MASAE/Shutterstock Images, p. 30 (flag); Benjamin Kralj/Shutterstock Images, p. 27 (bottom); D. Ribeiro/Shutterstock Images, p. 19; damienjkennedyphotography/Shutterstock Images, p. 25; Derek Brumby/iStockphoto, p. 13; Diarmuid Greene/Shutterstock Images, p. 6 (bottom); Everett Collection/Shutterstock Images, p. 28 (bottom right); Featureflash Photo Agency/Shutterstock Images, p. 23; Fireglo/Shutterstock Images, p. 26 (left); The Hornbills Studio/Shutterstock Images, p. 7 (map); Jennifer Boyer/Flickr, p. 27 (top right); kovop58/Shutterstock Images, p. 29 (top); luciann.photography/Shutterstock Images, p. 6 (top); lukulo/iStockphoto, pp. 5 (compass), 7 (compass); Maryna Pleshkun/Shutterstock Images, p. 30 (currency); Natalia Paklina/Shutterstock Images, p. 17; Panaspics/Shutterstock Images, p. 26 (right); Pyty/Shutterstock Images, p. 5 (map); Salvador Maniquiz/Shutterstock Images, p. 28 (bottom left); seanfitz09/Shutterstock Images, p. 9; shawnwil23/Shutterstock Images, p. 27 (top left); Thoom/Shutterstock Images, p. 28 (top); Tom Rose/Shutterstock Images, p. 21; webstoodio/Shutterstock Images, p. 15; Wikimedia Commons, pp. 11, 29 (bottom)
Design Elements: Mighty Media, Inc.
Country population and area figures taken from the CIA World Factbook

Library of Congress Control Number: 2022940508

Publisher's Cataloging-in-Publication Data

Names: Van, R.L., author.
Title: Ireland / by R.L. Van
Description: Minneapolis, Minnesota : Abdo Publishing, 2023 | Series: Countries | Includes online resources and index.
Identifiers: ISBN 9781532199646 (lib. bdg.) | ISBN 9781098274849 (ebook)
Subjects: LCSH: Ireland--Juvenile literature. | Europe--Juvenile literature. | Great Britain--History--Juvenile literature. | Ireland--History--Juvenile literature. | Geography--Juvenile literature.
Classification: DDC 941.5--dc23

CONTENTS

PASSPORT TO IRELAND

Ireland is in western Europe. It is on an island in the Atlantic Ocean. About 5.3 million people live there.

DID YOU KNOW?

Ocean winds cause many rainy days in Ireland.

WHERE IS IRELAND?
N
W
E
S
United Kingdom
Irish Sea
Atlantic Ocean
IRELAND
Celtic Sea

IMPORTANT CITIES

Dublin is Ireland's **capital** and largest city. It has a long history. It is a center of business, education, finance, and culture.

Cork is Ireland's second-largest city. It is known for its history, culture, and food.

Limerick is Ireland's third-largest city. It has many historical landmarks and is known for its culture.

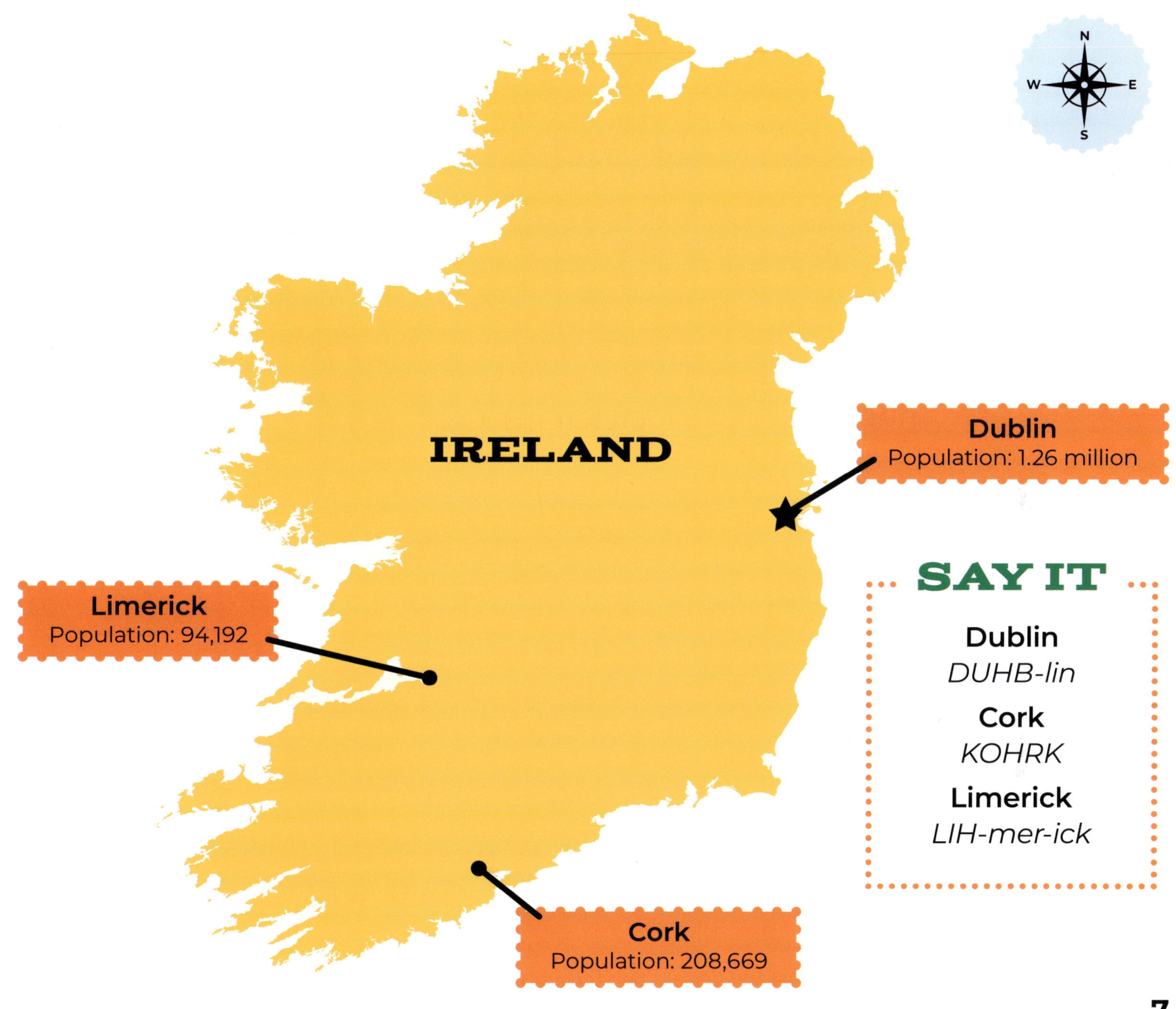

IRELAND
Dublin
Population: 1.26 million
Limerick
Population: 94,192
Cork
Population: 208,669
N
W
E
S

SAY IT
Dublin
DUHB-lin
Cork
KOHRK
Limerick
LIH-mer-ick

IRELAND IN HISTORY

Ireland's first people came from mainland Europe thousands of years ago. Over time, settlers built homes and monuments. By 300 BCE, **Celtic** tribes had settled the land. Many groups controlled Ireland over the years. In the 1500s, England gained full control.

Poulnabrone dolmen is a large, prehistoric tomb in County Clare, Ireland. It was built between 4200 and 2900 BCE.

In 1801, Ireland became part of the United Kingdom. But many Irish people wanted independence. The War for Irish Independence began in 1919.

In 1920, Ireland split into two parts. Northern Ireland remained part of the United Kingdom. The rest of Ireland became independent. In 1949, it became the Republic of Ireland.

British forces set the city of Cork on fire during the War for Irish Independence.

AN IMPORTANT SYMBOL

Ireland's flag has three stripes. Green is for Roman **Catholics**. Orange is for **Protestants**. White is the hope for peace between them.

Ireland is a **parliamentary republic**. The president is head of state. The prime minister is head of government. Parliament makes laws.

The Irish flag was first flown in 1848.

ACROSS THE LAND

Ireland has farmland, wetlands, and forests. Mountains and rocky cliffs rise along the coasts. The weather is usually mild and rainy.

Foxes, hedgehogs, badgers, and many types of birds and fish live in Ireland. Grasses, heath, moss, and some trees grow there.

Killarney National Park was Ireland's first national park.

EARNING A LIVING

Ireland's factories make medicines, food products, and computer parts. Most Irish people have service jobs.

Ireland is a leading producer of lead and zinc. Fish and shellfish come from its seas. Farmers grow hay, grains, sugar beets, and potatoes. They raise livestock for meat.

Many Irish sheep farmers
allow their flocks to
roam the countryside.

LIFE IN IRELAND

Most Irish people live in cities. Traditional Irish foods include potatoes, soda bread, Irish stew, and corned beef.

The Irish enjoy horse racing, soccer, Gaelic football, rugby, and **hurling**. Most people in Ireland are Roman **Catholic**.

In Ireland, soccer is called "football." The Republic of Ireland's national team plays in Dublin.

FAMOUS FACES

Niall Horan was born in Mullingar, Ireland. In 2010, he joined the boy band One Direction. Two years later, the band's first album sold millions of copies worldwide. Horan started a successful solo music career in 2016. He is involved in several charities.

SAY IT

Niall Horan
NYE-uhl HAW-ren

Niall Horan was the only member of One Direction who was not born in England.

Saoirse Ronan was born in New York City to Irish parents. She grew up in Dublin. At age 12, she got her first major acting role. She has since starred in many movies, including *Little Women*. Ronan has received many award **nominations** for her work.

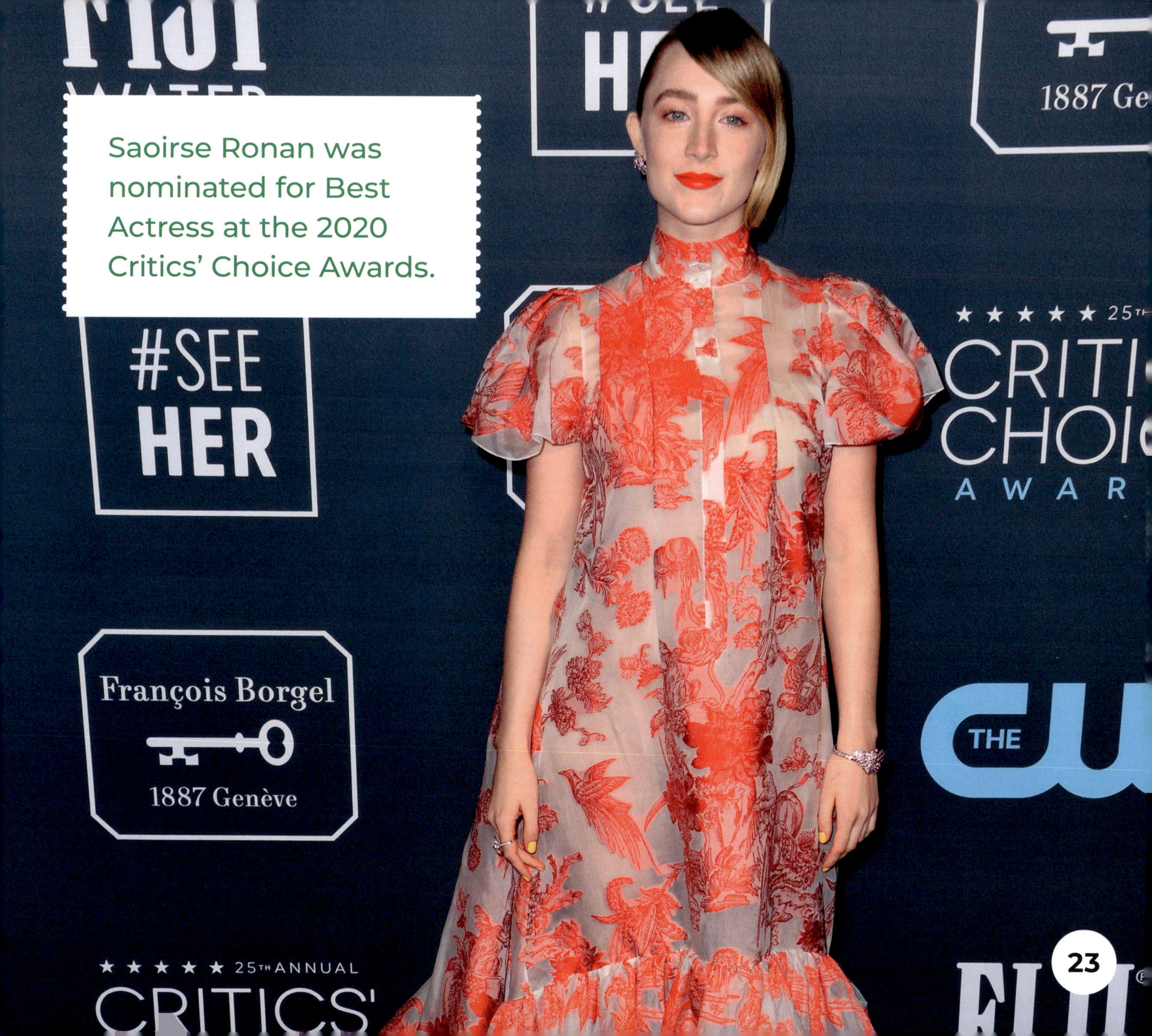

Saoirse Ronan was nominated for Best Actress at the 2020 Critics' Choice Awards.

A GREAT COUNTRY

Ireland is a land of green hills and historic castles. Ireland's people and places help make the world a more interesting place.

There are more than
30,000 castles in Ireland.
Classiebawn Castle sits on
the country's northern coast.

TOUR BOOK

If you ever visit Ireland, here are some places to go and things to do!

EXPLORE

Visit Phoenix Park in Dublin, the largest enclosed urban park in Europe.

DISCOVER

Explore one of Ireland's many castles, such as Kilkenny Castle.

SEE

Walk a trail through Ireland's forests. Some people claim that fairies live there!

SMOOCH

Kiss the Blarney Stone at Blarney Castle near Cork for good luck.

REMEMBER

Learn about Ireland's fight for independence at Kilmainham Gaol, a famous jail in Dublin.

TIMELINE

AROUND 432

Saint Patrick arrived in Ireland to teach people about **Christianity**.

1592

Trinity College Dublin, Ireland's oldest university, was started.

1845

The Irish Potato Famine began. About 1 million people died from hunger, and millions more left the country.

1916

The Easter Rising
took place in Dublin.
Irish **rebels** fought
for freedom from the
United Kingdom.

2020

Ireland won two gold medals at
the Tokyo Summer Olympics,
the most since 1996.

1949

The Republic of
Ireland began
on April 18.

1990

Mary Robinson became the
first female president of Ireland.

IRELAND
UP CLOSE

Official Name
Éire (Ireland)

Flag

Population
5,275,004 (2022 est.)
123rd-most-populated country

Total Area
27,133 square miles
(70,273 sq km)
119th-largest country

Official Languages
English, Irish

Capital
Dublin

Currency
Euro

Form of Government
Parliamentary republic

National Anthem
"Amhran na bhFiann" ("The Soldier's Song")

GLOSSARY

capital—a city where government leaders meet.

Catholic—a member of the Roman Catholic Church. This kind of Christianity has been around since the first century and is led by the pope.

Celtic (KEHL-tihk)—relating to a group of people who lived about 2,000 years ago in many countries of western Europe.

Christianity—a religion based on the teachings of Jesus Christ.

hurling—a game that is similar to field hockey. It is played between two teams of 15 players each.

nomination—a suggestion that a person receive a certain honor or position.

parliamentary republic—a government that has a leader who is usually a president, not a king or queen, and a parliament that makes laws.

Protestant—a Christian who does not belong to the Catholic Church.

rebel—a person who resists authority.

ONLINE RESOURCES

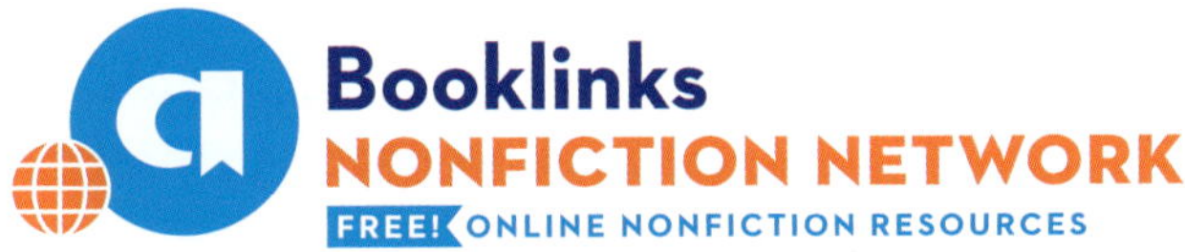

To learn more about Ireland, please visit **abdobooklinks.com** or scan this QR code. These links are routinely monitored and updated to provide the most current information available.

INDEX